TOP 10
FASTEST

Ruth Owen

A cheetah

🌳 Crabtree Publishing Company

www.crabtreebooks.com

Crabtree Publishing Company

www.crabtreebooks.com   1-800-387-7650

PMB 59051   616 Welland Avenue,
350 Fifth Avenue, 59th Floor   St. Catharines, Ontario
New York, NY, 10118   L2M 5V6

Content development by   Published by
Shakespeare Squared   Crabtree Publishing
                          Company © 2010
www.ShakespeareSquared.com
                          First published
No part of this publication may   in Great Britain in
be reproduced, copied, stored in 2010 by TickTock
a retrieval system or transmitted in   Entertainment Ltd.
any form or by any means electronic,
mechanical, photocopying, recording   Printed in the
or otherwise without prior written   U.S.A./122009
permission of the copyright owner.   CG20091120

Crabtree Publishing
Company credits:
Project manager: Kathy Middleton
Editor: Reagan Miller
Proofreader: Crystal Sikkens
Production coordinator: Katherine Berti
Prepress technician: Katherine Berti

TickTock credits:
Publisher: Melissa Fairley
Art director: Faith Booker
Editor: Victoria Garrard
Designer: Emma Randall
Production controller: Ed Green
Production manager: Suzy Kelly

Thank you to Lorraine Petersen and the members of nasen

Picture credits (t=top; b=bottom; c=centre; l=left; r=right; OFC=outside front cover): Image courtesy of the Australian National Maritime Museum: Spirit of Australia is part of the museum's collection: 16–17, 29cl. Bloodhound SSC: 7. iStock: 1, 12–13, 24–25, 26t, 26b, 28bl, 29tl. NASA/courtesy of nasaimages.com: 18–19, 29br. Emily Nathan/Getty Images: 23b. Shutterstock: 4, 5r, 14–15, 22, 23t, 27, 28tl, 28tr, 31. Skyscan Photolibrary/Alamy: 6, 29bl. Courtesy of SSC: 4–5bc, 8–9, 29tr. Keren Su/Corbis: 20–21, 29cr. Suzuki GB Plc: OFC, 2, 10–11, 28br. © 2008 QWSR Ltd./Spline Design: 17t.

Every effort has been made to trace copyright holders, and we apologize in advance for any omissions. We would be pleased to insert the appropriate acknowledgments in any subsequent edition of this publication.

Library and Archives Canada Cataloguing in Publication

Owen, Ruth, 1967-
    Top 10 fastest / Ruth Owen.

(Crabtree contact)
Includes index.
ISBN 978-0-7787-7488-4 (bound).--ISBN 978-0-7787-7509-6 (pbk.)

        1. Speed--Juvenile literature. I. Title.
II. Title: Top ten fastest. III. Series: Crabtree contact

QC137.52.O94 2010   j531'.112   C2009-906466-9

Library of Congress Cataloging-in-Publication Data

Owen, Ruth, 1967-
 Top 10 fastest / Ruth Owen.
     p. cm. -- (Crabtree contact)
 Includes index.
 ISBN 978-0-7787-7488-4 (reinforced lib. bdg. : alk. paper) --
 ISBN 978-0-7787-7509-6 (pbk. : alk. paper)
 1. Speed--Juvenile literature. I. Title. II. Title: Top ten fastest. III.
 Series.

 QC137.52.O944 2010
 531'.112--dc22

                                          2009044258

The 2008
Suzuki Hayabusa

CONTENTS

INTRODUCTION

This book is all about the world's fastest things.

From **fast** machines...
...to **fast** birds...
...to **fast** cars, planes, and motorbikes.

The peregrine falcon is the fastest bird on Earth. It can dive at a speed of 200 miles per hour (322 kilometers per hour).

Taipei 101 is 1,666 feet (508 meters) tall. The super fast elevators carry passengers to the top in just 30 seconds!

The *Ultimate Aero* is the world's fastest supercar. It has a top speed of 257 miles per hour (414 kilometers per hour).

WORLD LAND SPEED RECORD

For over 100 years people have tried to travel the fastest on land.

The world land speed record is held by *Thrust SSC*. SSC stands for **SuperSonic** Car.

In 1997, *Thrust* went supersonic—faster than the **speed of sound**. It reached 763 miles per hour (1,228 kilometers per hour)!

Thrust SSC

A team of engineers are planning to beat this record. They are building *Bloodhound SSC*.

Bloodhound SSC will be powered by a jet engine and rockets.

Bloodhound SSC

Richard Noble is the project director.

Andy Green will drive the car.

In 2011, *Bloodhound SSC* will try to go faster than 994 miles per hour (1,600 kilometers per hour).

FASTEST CAR

The *Ultimate Aero* is the world's fastest production car. This means it is a car that is produced for use on normal roads.

The *Ultimate Aero* is in the **Guinness Book of World Records™**. The car made two test runs in front of officials from Guinness in order to earn the title of the fastest car.

It reached 257 miles per hour (414 kilometers per hour) on its first test run and 255 miles per hour (410 kilometers per hour) on its second test run.

The two speeds were averaged to determine the record-breaking speed of 256 miles per hour (412.28 kilometers per hour).

Ultimate Aero Specs:
- Made by Shelby Supercars in Washington state
- Top speed: 257 miles per hour (414 kilometers per hour)
- Can do 0 to 60 miles per hour (97 kilometers per hour) in 2.78 seconds

FASTEST MOTORBIKE

The world's fastest, most powerful motorbike is the *2008 Suzuki™ Hayabusa*.

It can reach speeds of nearly 200 miles per hour (322 kilometers per hour). The bike can go faster than this, but for safety reasons its speed is restricted.

2008 Suzuki™ Hayabusa

FASTEST BIRD

The peregrine falcon is the fastest bird on Earth. It can dive on prey at more than 200 miles per hour (322 kilometers per hour).

The Hayabusa, the fastest motorbike in the world, was named after the peregrine falcon. The word "hayabus" is Japanese for peregrine falcon.

The peregrine falcon mainly eats medium-sized birds. They also hunt for small **mammals**, reptiles, and even insects.

The male and female look very similar, but the female is much bigger than the male.

peregrine falcon

FASTEST ELEVATOR

The world's fastest elevators travel upward at 56 feet per second (17 meters per second).

The elevators are in Taipei 101, a building in the city of Taipei on the Chinese island of Taiwan. Taipei 101 is one of the tallest buildings in the world. It is 1,666 feet (508 meters) tall.

The elevators are fitted with a special pressure system. This system stops the ears of passengers from popping!

WATER SPEED RECORD

For nearly 100 years people have tried to be the fastest on water.

The world water speed record is 317.6 miles per hour (511 kilometers per hour).

This record was set in 1978 by an Australian man named Ken Warby. The boat was called *Spirit of Australia*.

Spirit of Australia

Quicksilver

A team of British engineers want to break this record. They are building a boat named *Quicksilver*, driven by Nigel Macknight.

Quicksilver will try to break the water speed record in 2012.

FASTEST AIRCRAFT

The *X-43A* is the fastest jet-powered aircraft. It is an experimental **aircraft and was built by scientists at** NASA.

The X-43A was built using new technology. It is designed to take in air from the **atmosphere** and combine it with fuel to power the aircraft. Scientists believe this technology will allow planes to fly at thousands of miles per hour.

X-43A

The *X-43A* does not have a pilot. It is launched from a *B-52B* plane. A booster rocket then launches the *X-43A*. Once it's released from the rocket, the *X-43A*'s engine takes over!

In 2004, the *X-43A* reached a speed of nearly 7,000 miles per hour (11,265 kilometers per hour).

FASTEST TRAIN

The fastest type of train in the world is the Maglev train. Its name stands for **"magnetic** levitation**."**

Maglev train

Magnets are used to lift the train above a special track. Magnets are also used to guide and move the train.

The world's only **commercial** Maglev railway is in China. Several other countries have plans to build their own Maglev trains.

The fastest speed recorded for a Maglev train is 361 miles per hour (581 kilometers per hour). This was during a test run in Japan.

FASTEST GROWING PLANT

Bamboo is a woody, evergreen **type of grass. It is the fastest growing plant in the world.**

There are around 1,000 different types of bamboo. Some types can grow up to 3.28 feet (one meter) in a single day!

Bamboo is very strong. It can be used as a building material.

A temple in Indonesia being built from bamboo.

Bamboo can be used to make all sorts of things including clothes and cutlery.

FASTEST MAMMAL

The world's fastest mammal is the cheetah. Over a short distance a cheetah can run at 70.2 miles per hour (113 kilometers per hour).

Every part of a cheetah's body is designed for speed:

- Large nostrils and lungs to take in more air
- A long, streamlined body and thin bones
- Special paw pads and claws to help push off from the ground
- A spine which works as a spring for the powerful back legs

ANIMAL SPEED FREAKS

The fastest water mammals are orcas and Dall porpoises. They can swim at up to 34.8 miles per hour (56 kilometers per hour).

orca

Dall porpoise

Ostriches are the fastest birds on land. They can run at 44.7 miles per hour (72 kilometers per hour).

ostrich

TOP 10 FASTEST

Some of the fastest things on Earth were created by nature. Others were built by people.

They are all amazing record-breakers.

10

Fastest growing plant: bamboo

Bamboo can grow up to 3.28 feet (one meter) per day.

9

Fastest elevator: Taipei 101

56 feet per second (17 meters per second)

8

Fastest mammal: Cheetah

70.2 miles per hour (113 kilometers per hour)

7

Fastest motorbike: 2008 Suzuki™ Hayabusa

200 miles per hour (322 kilometers per hour)

6

Fastest bird:
peregrine falcon

200 miles per hour
(322 kilometers per hour)

5

Fastest production car:
Ultimate Aero

257 miles per hour
(414 kilometers per hour)

4

Fastest boat:
Spirit of Australia,

317.6 miles per hour
(511 kilometers per hour)

3

Fastest train:
Maglev train

361 miles per hour
(581 kilometers per hour)

2

Fastest on land:
Thrust SSC

763 miles per hour
(1,228 kilometers per hour)

1

Fastest aircraft:
X-43A

7,000 miles per hour
(11,265 kilometers per hour)

NEED-TO-KNOW WORDS

atmosphere
The entire mass of air surrounding Earth

commercial
Something that is created and available to the public

evergreen A type of plant that has leaves all year long

experimental
Something that is part of an experiment, or something that is being tried out or tested

Guinness Book of World Records™
An organization that records and measures record-breaking things and events. The world records are then published in a book each year

levitation When something rises and floats in the air

mammal An animal with fur or hair on its body. A mammal's body temperature stays the same no matter how hot or cold the air or water is around it

NASA (National Aeronautics and Space Administration) NASA is an organization of the American government that runs the U.S. space program

speed of sound
Sound is a vibration. In air, that vibration travels at about 760 miles per hour (1,223 kilometers per hour). It is about four times as fast in water

supersonic Faster than the speed of sound

SUPERSONIC AIRLINER

- *Concorde* is the world's only supersonic commercial airliner.

- It flew at around 1,348 miles per hour (2,169 kilometers per hour). That is almost twice the speed of sound.

Concorde

- A *Concorde* could fly from London to New York in around three hours 20 minutes. A *Boeing 747* takes more than seven hours to make the trip.

- Between 1976 and 2003, 2.5 million passengers traveled on *Concorde*.

- The fleet of *Concordes* is no longer flying. No other supersonic commercial airliner has replaced them.

FIND OUT MORE ONLINE

Learn more about aerodynamics.
www.bloodhoundssc.com

Find out more about the Ultimate Aero.
www.shelbysupercars.com/car-specs.php

Find additional information about the world water speed record.
www.quicksilver-wsr.com

Publisher's note to educators and parents:
Our editors have carefully reviewed these web sites to ensure that they are suitable for children. Many websites change frequently, however, and we cannot guarantee that a site's future contents will continue to meet our high standards of quality and educational value. Be advised that children should be closely supervised whenever they access the Internet.

INDEX